Where it all began

'Reading Roy' outside 12 High Street, Old Portsmouth.

On a Tuesday evening 5th April 1898, a group of five businessmen met at 12 High Street, Old Portsmouth.

It was proposed that a plot of land close to Goldsmith Avenue be purchased to build a football ground for 'The Portsmouth Football and Athletic Company Ltd'.

This was the birth of 'Pompey'.

Over the next century the club would become one of the most famous in England and their fans some of the most passionate and loyal.

Pompey Pubs

- The Meon
- The Electric Arms
- The Magpie
- The Connaught Arms
- The Newcome Arms
- The Good Companion
- The Pickwick
- The Brewers Arms
- The Travellers Joy
- The Shepherds Crook
- Froddington Arms
- The Rutland Arms
- The Devonshire Arms
- The White House
- The Milton Arms
- The Rose in June

The Connaught Arms

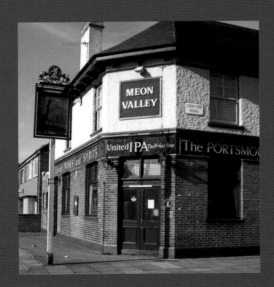

The Meon

The Electric Arms

The Magpie

The Good Companion

The Newcome Arms

The Pickwick

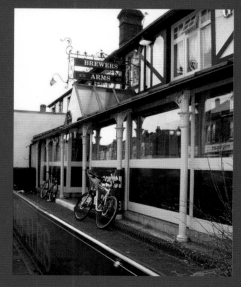

The Brewers Arms

The Travellers Joy

The Shepherds Crook

The Rutland Arms

The Froddington Arms

The Devonshire Arms

The Rose in June

The White House

The Barn

The Milton Arms

LEAGUE DIVISION ONE
You are advised to take up your position half an hour before the kick-off.
STANDING ONLY
TICKET No.
1540
W.J.B. DAVIS
Company Secretary
For date and other details
PORTSMOUTH F.C.
FRATTON PARK, PORTSMOUTH
V
MANCHESTER UNITED
COCA-COLA CUP
5TH ROUND REPLAY
Wednesday 26th January 1994
KICK OFF 7.45 P.M.
STANDING ONLY
Ticket No
07031
TERRACE
MILTON LANE TURNSTILES
TOTTENHAM HOTSPUR
4TH ROUND/2ND REPLAY
PORTSMOUTH FC
FRATTON PARK
CONCESSIONARY
ADULT

Pompey at Home

Toilet wall graffiti

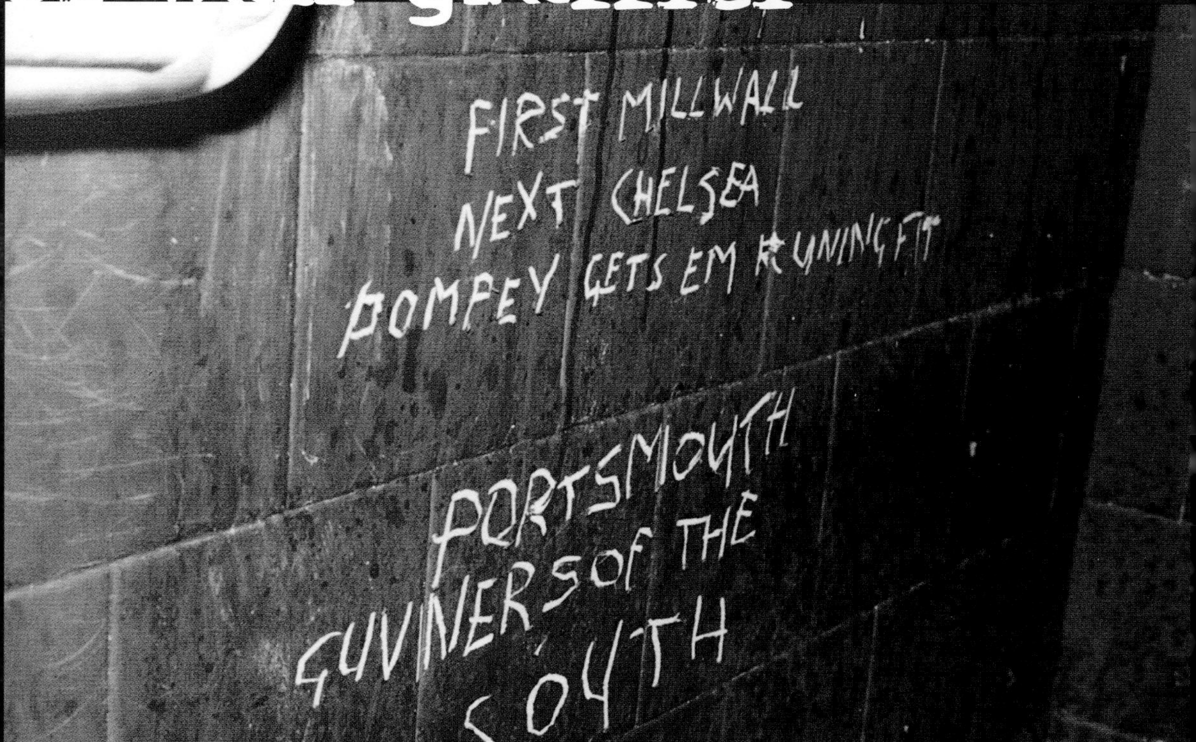

FIRST MILLWALL
NEXT CHELSEA
POMPEY GETS EM RUNING FIT

PORTSMOUTH
GUVNERS OF THE
SOUTH

Huddersfield Town 1980

Under the South Stand

Pompey mob under the South Stand

Pompey waiting for Huddersfield in Apsley Road

Pompey lads on the Milton End

Pre-match at the station

Going off at the station

Leeds outside the ground

Leeds weighing up the options

Trouble in Frogmore Road

Southend United 1983
Promotion to Division 2

Ginger and Frank

CHAAARGE!

Southend United 1983
Promotion to Division 2

Bobby Campbell and friends

Pete, Ricky and Duck

Scum 1984
F.A. Cup 4th Round

Goldsmith Avenue

Pre-match in The Robert Peel in Somerstown

Walking through Somerstown

Meathead - behind enemy lines

A packed Fratton End

Scummers on the Milton End and the gap they say never existed

Scum 1984 - F.A. Cup 4th Round

Ted getting nicked

Sheffield United 1987
Promotion to Division 1

Sheffield United 1987
Promotion to Division 1

Sheffield United 1987
Promotion to Division 1

Away Days

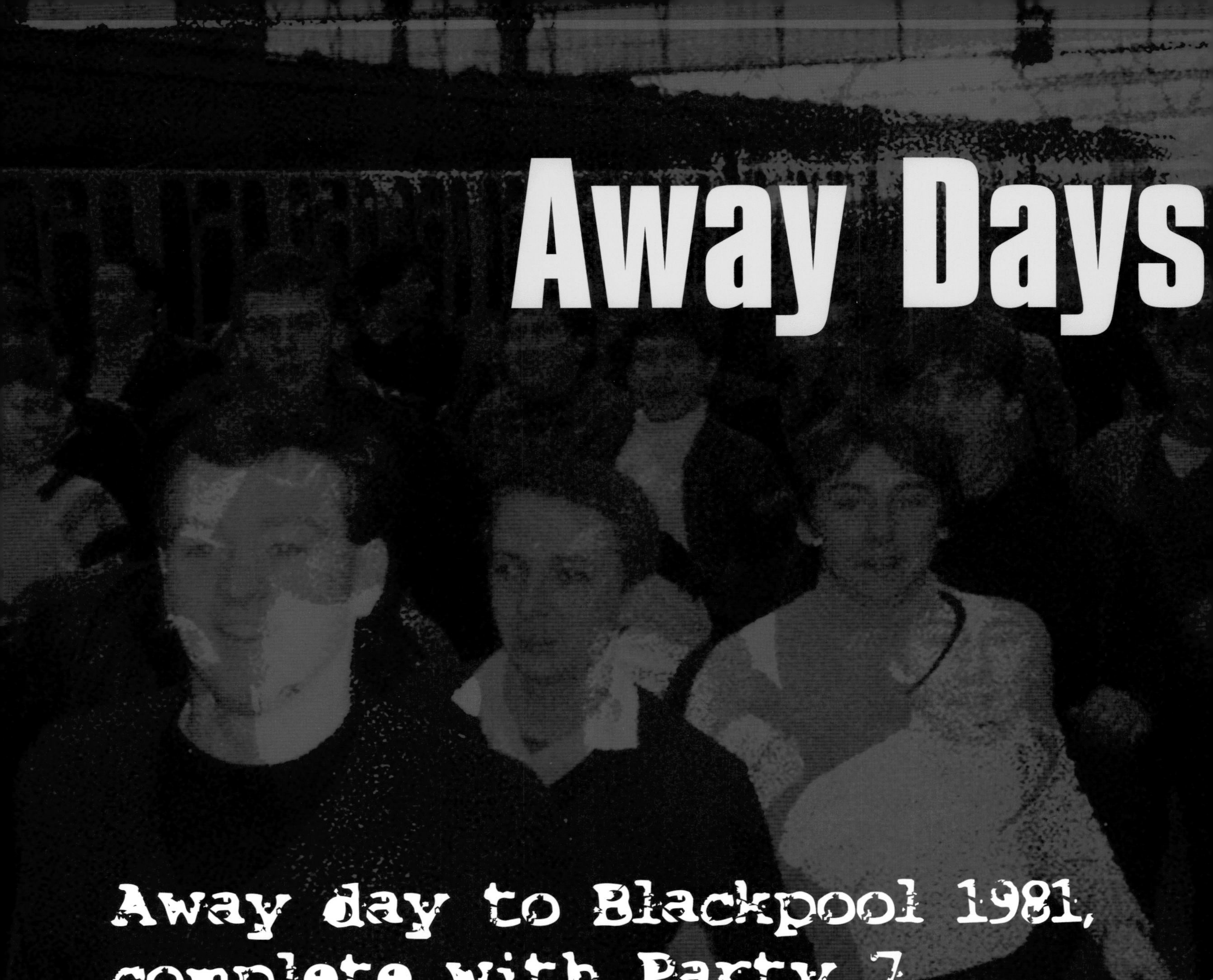

Away day to Blackpool 1981, complete with Party 7.

Northampton Town 1980 -
Promotion from Division 4

Wimbledon 1978

The Stamshaw Boys in fancy dress set off for London

Millwall 1980

The Boys outside The Ship Anson before getting the train to Millwall

Pompey outside The Den

Scott, Mark and Reading Roy

Fooksie trying to get the lads back on the train

Liverpool - League Cup 4th Round 1980
12,000 Pompey fans travel to Anfield

The Stamshaw Boys on the way to Liverpool

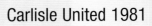

Blackpool 1981

Pompey at Blackpool

In the pub at Bristol

Bristol City centre

Chesterfield 1982

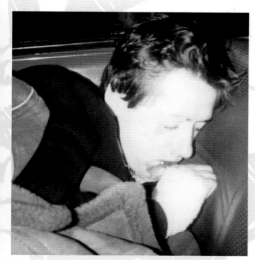

Bad day for Maysie

Swansea City 1983

Wrexham 1983

Brighton and Hove Albion 1983

Brighton away by pushbike

Millwall 1983

E.C. woz 'ere

Pompey at Waterloo

Tear gased at London Bridge

Millwall 1983

Ethel posing!

Pompey in Millwall's seats

In Millwall's seats - and never moved!

Come on Millwall!

Pompey escort back to the station

Bournemouth 1983

Leeds 1983

On route to Leeds Pompey fans stopped the train at Wakefield to escape the police escort

Pompey at Wakefield Cathedral

Cardiff City 1983

Chelsea 1983

Chelsea 1983

Sheffield United 1983

Plymouth Argyle 1983
Pompey Division 3 Champions

Stamshaw Boys on tour

Plymouth Argyle 1983
Pompey Division 3 Champions

Plymouth Argyle 1983
Pompey Division 3 Champions

Cambridge United 1984

The Boys took bikes across London and on to Cambridge for an away day with a difference

The lads turned up at Cardiff suited and booted, they told the police they were going to a wedding and were left un-escorted

Birmingham City 1984

Running Brum from their seats

Barnsley 1984

Meeting Leeds on the train going home…OUCH!

Middlesbrough 1984

Charlton Athletic 1984

Pompey mob at London Bridge

The mob who ran Leicester

Going off with Leicester near Picadilly Circus before the game

Manchester City 1984

Rucking with City before the game

Steve Rogers…well it was the 80's!

Oxford United 1984

Wolverhampton Wanderers 1985

Sunderland 1985

Portsmouth v Leicester City, 1st Division play off. Fratton Park 1993.

Tottenham Hotspur 1985

Going off after the game

Manchester City 1985

Pompey v Liverpool 1992
F.A. Cup Semi-final at Highbury

F.U.G. in the Highlands

Pompey v Liverpool 1992
F.A. Cup Semi-final at Highbury

Pompey v Liverpool 1992
F.A. Cup Semi-final replay at Villa Park

Pompey v Liverpool 1992
F.A. Cup Semi-final replay at Villa Park

Bari 1992 - Anglo Italian Cup

Notts County 1993

Leicester City 1994

Sunderland 1993

Coach from The Connaught Arms

Le Havre 1996 - pre-season friendly

Pompey played a pre-season friendly against french club Le Havre in 1996. Instead of playing at their stadium the game was played at a tiny ground in Honfleur. Pompey fans invaded the pitch as a protest of the way the club was being run by Gregory. The match was abandoned and the ferry on the way back was wrecked.

Preston North End 2003

Bradford City 2003
Division 1 Champions

Fareham F.U.G.

Dad's army

Wisp, Pete, Shaun, Ralphy and Coat

Bradford City 2003
Division 1 Champions

Pompey & England

England v Russia 1984

Pompey Boys at Glasgow Central

Milton Boys - 'Italia 90'

Albania v England 2001

Italy v England 1997

Fingers in the Olympic Stadium - Rome

England v Scotland 1996

World Cup - France 1998

Scummers - wrong place, wrong time?

The Gillen boys

Germany v England - Olympic Stadium, Munich 2001

Slovakia v England - Bratislava 2002

The Amsterdam Bar - 6.57 HQ

World Cup - Japan 2002

MGM GRAND
THE CITY OF ENTERTAINM
LAS VEGAS
PORTSMOUTH
SUPPORTERS CLUB

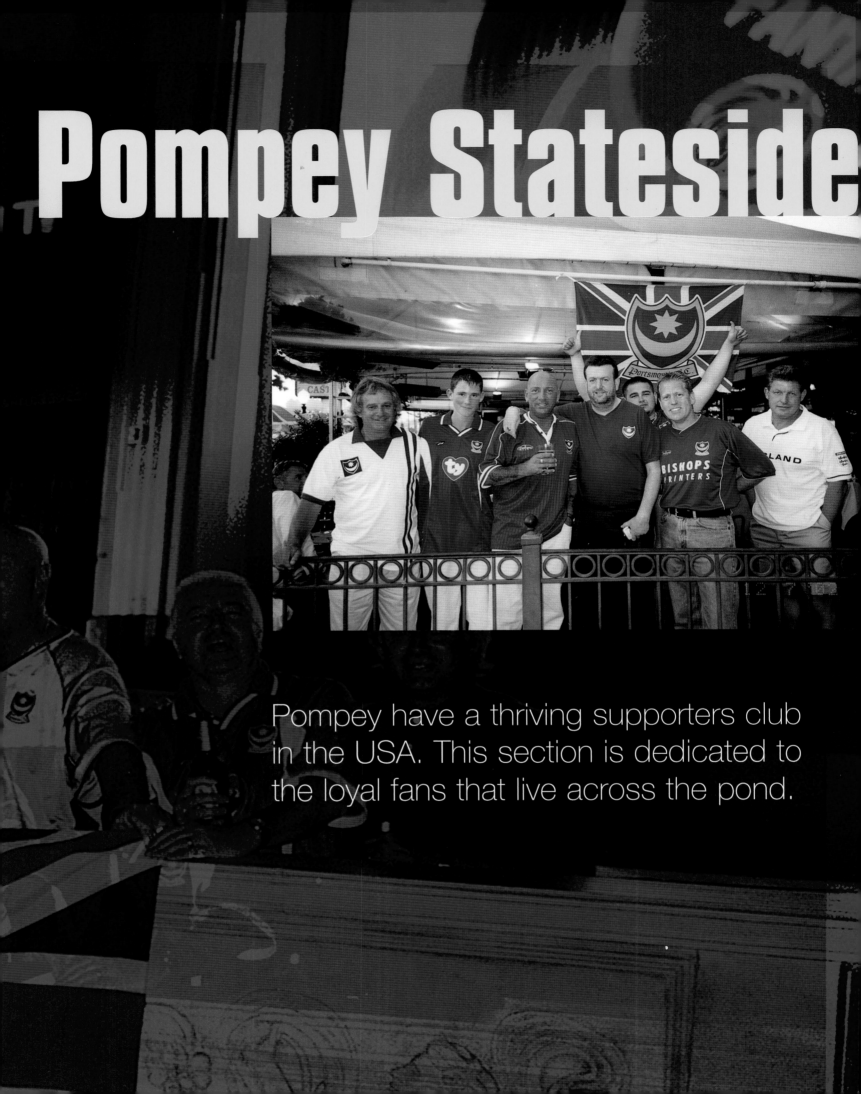

Pompey Stateside

Pompey have a thriving supporters club in the USA. This section is dedicated to the loyal fans that live across the pond.

Butch and Jonesy

Elvis Pompey

Jonesy and Harley

Butch and Jonesy - San Diego, California

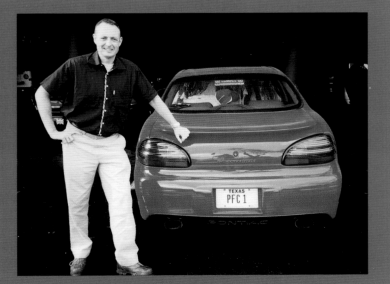

Wrighty

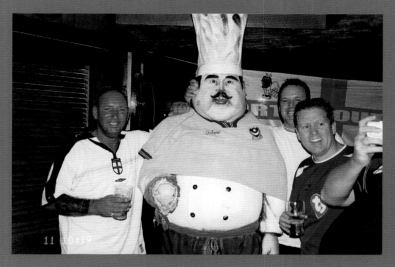

Butch, Micky Quinn, Neil and Jonesy

PFC USA Las Vegas 2002

Jonesy

The Pompey Boys

Pompey til I (nearly) died. Ritchie Rolfe - stabbed at Reading.

Dedicated to all the Pompey Boys, not only from the city but from Salisbury, Fareham, Gosport, Petersfield, Waterlooville, Havant, Leigh Park, Emsworth, Chichester, Bognor and further afield.

Pompey Loyal.

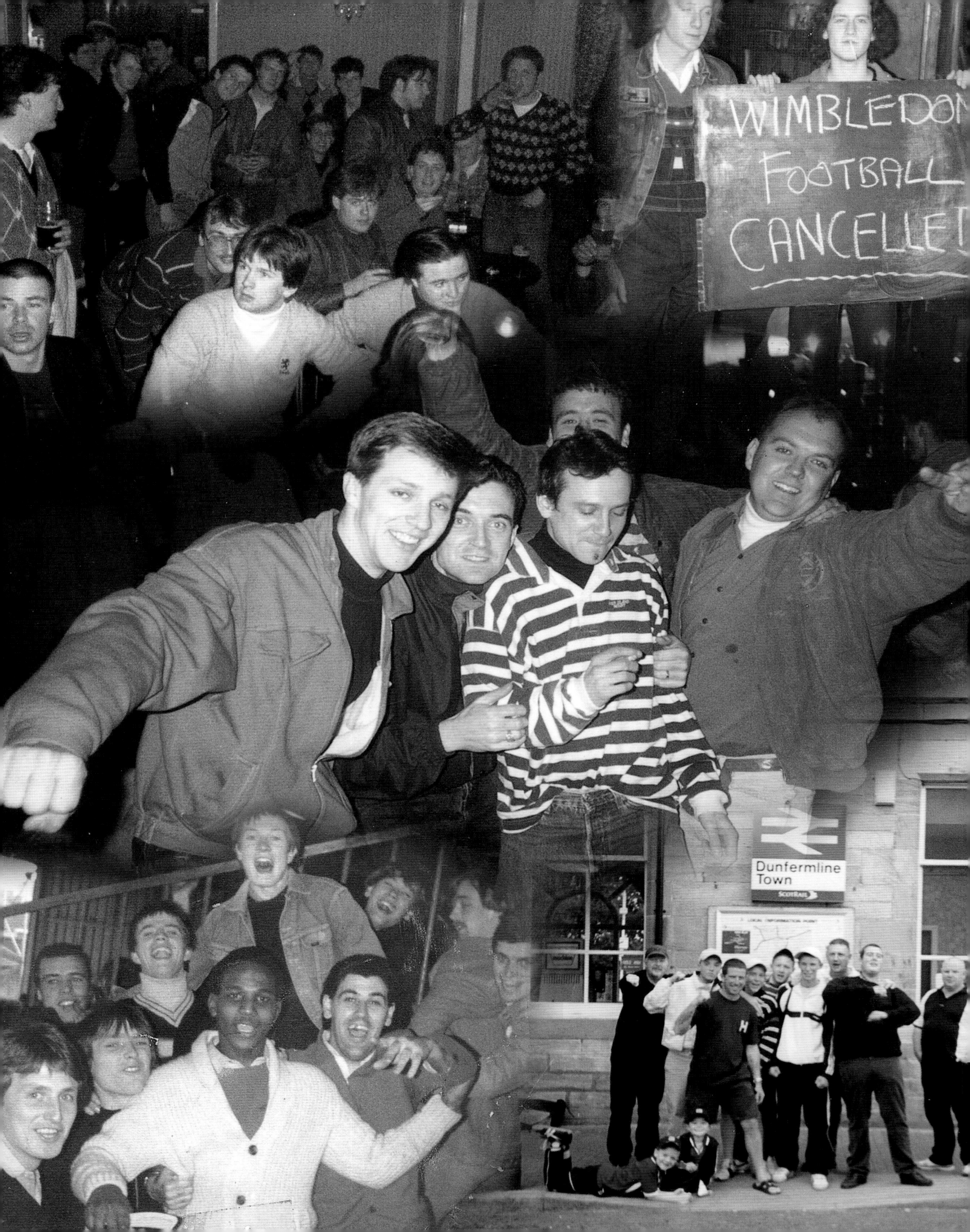
WIMBLEDON
FOOTBALL
CANCELLE
Dunfermline
Town
ScotRail

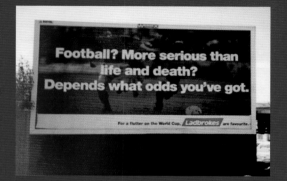

Football? More serious than
life and death?
Depends what odds you've got.

For a flutter on the World Cup. Ladbrokes are favourite..

PORTSMOUTH
F C

MotorWay
Tyres
Batteries
Exhausts

HASLEMERE ROAD   SAINTS ALWAYS RUN FROM POMPEY

NO ONE TAKES ON PORTSMOUTH
P.F.C.   "UP THE BLUES"

Branded

Pompey Tattoos

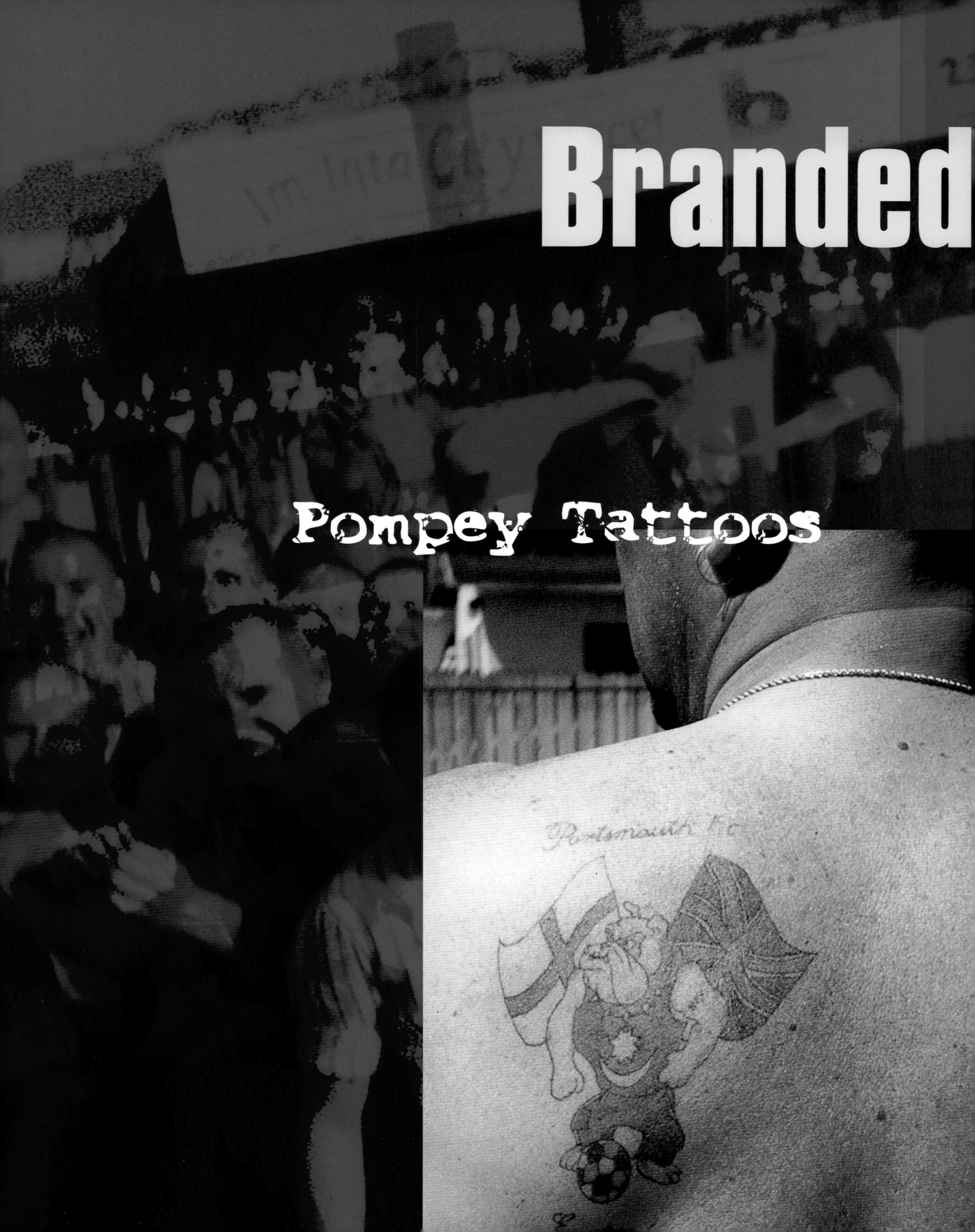

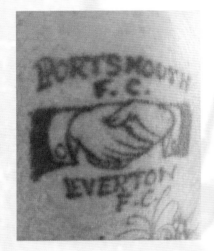

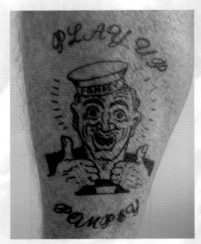

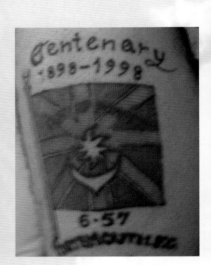
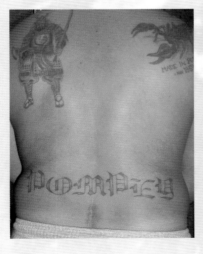

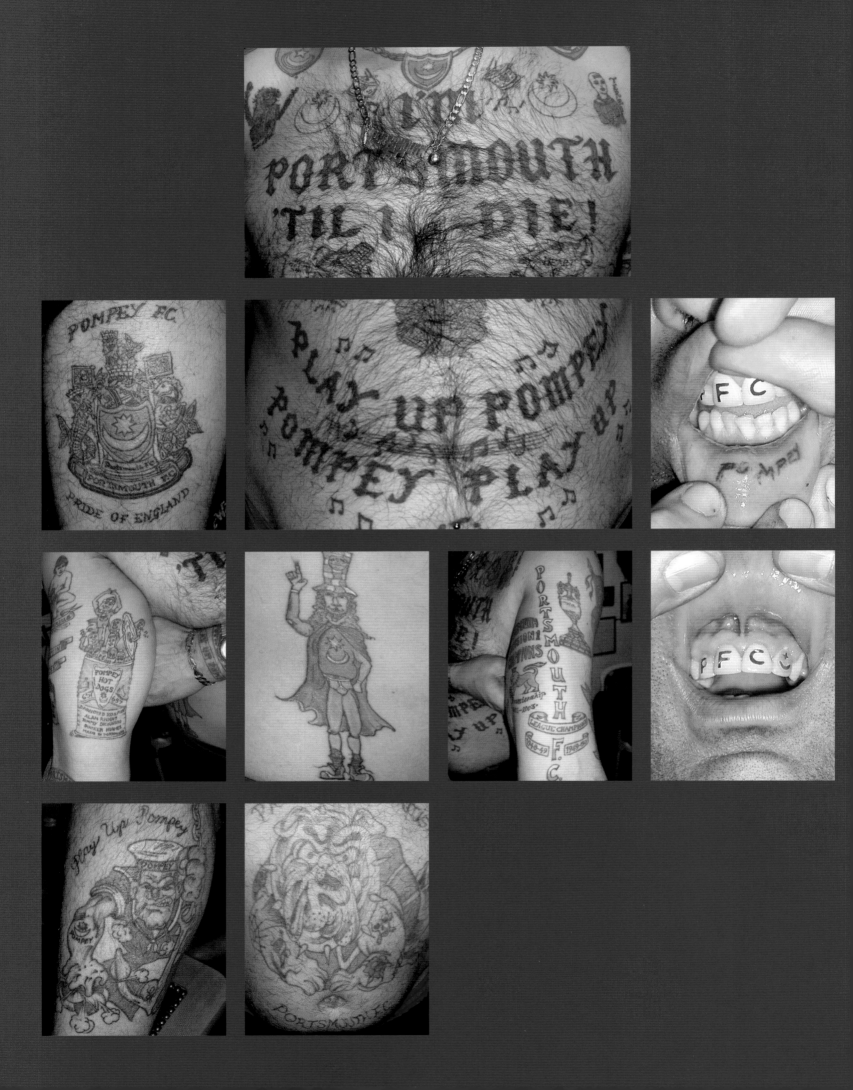

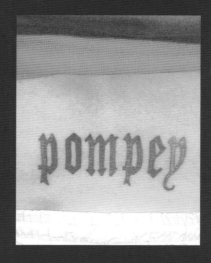

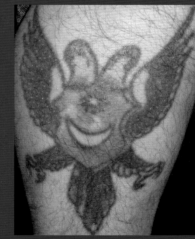

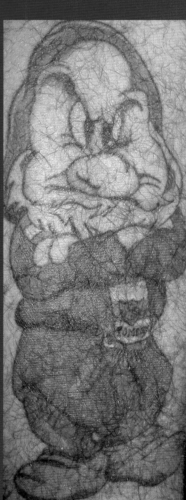

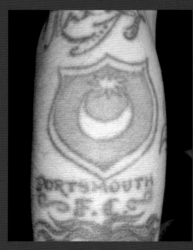

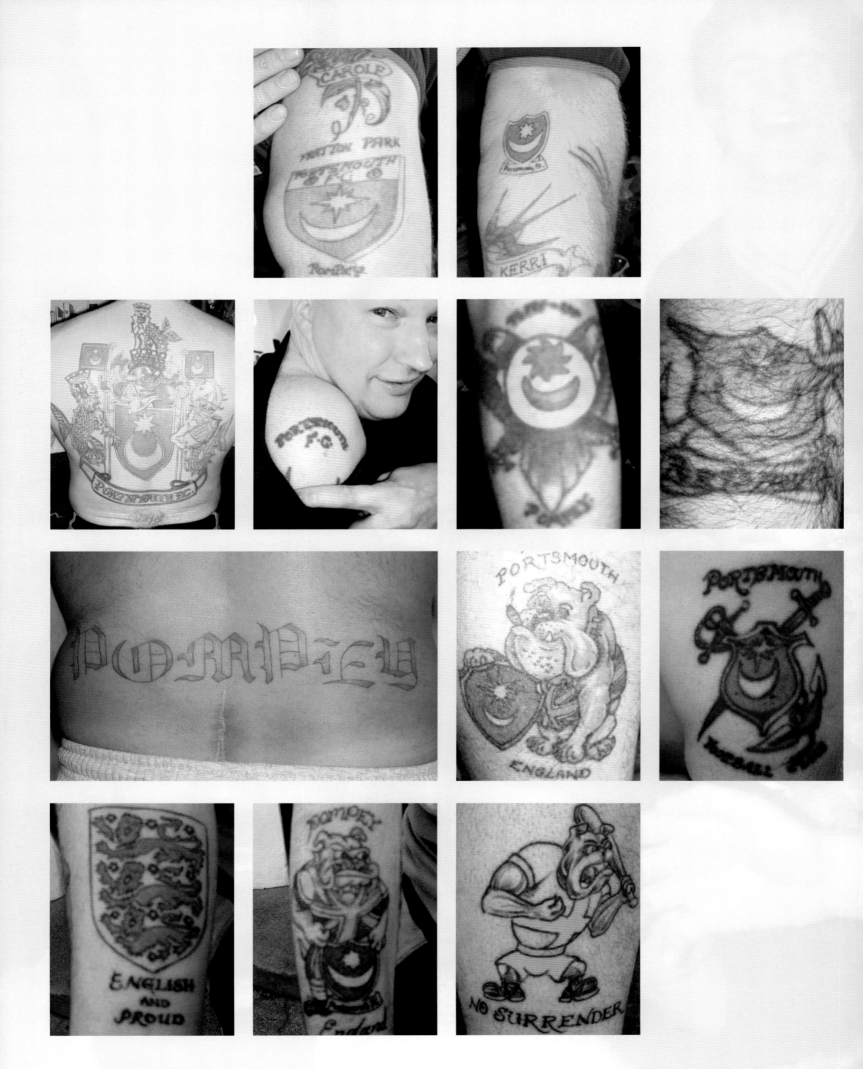

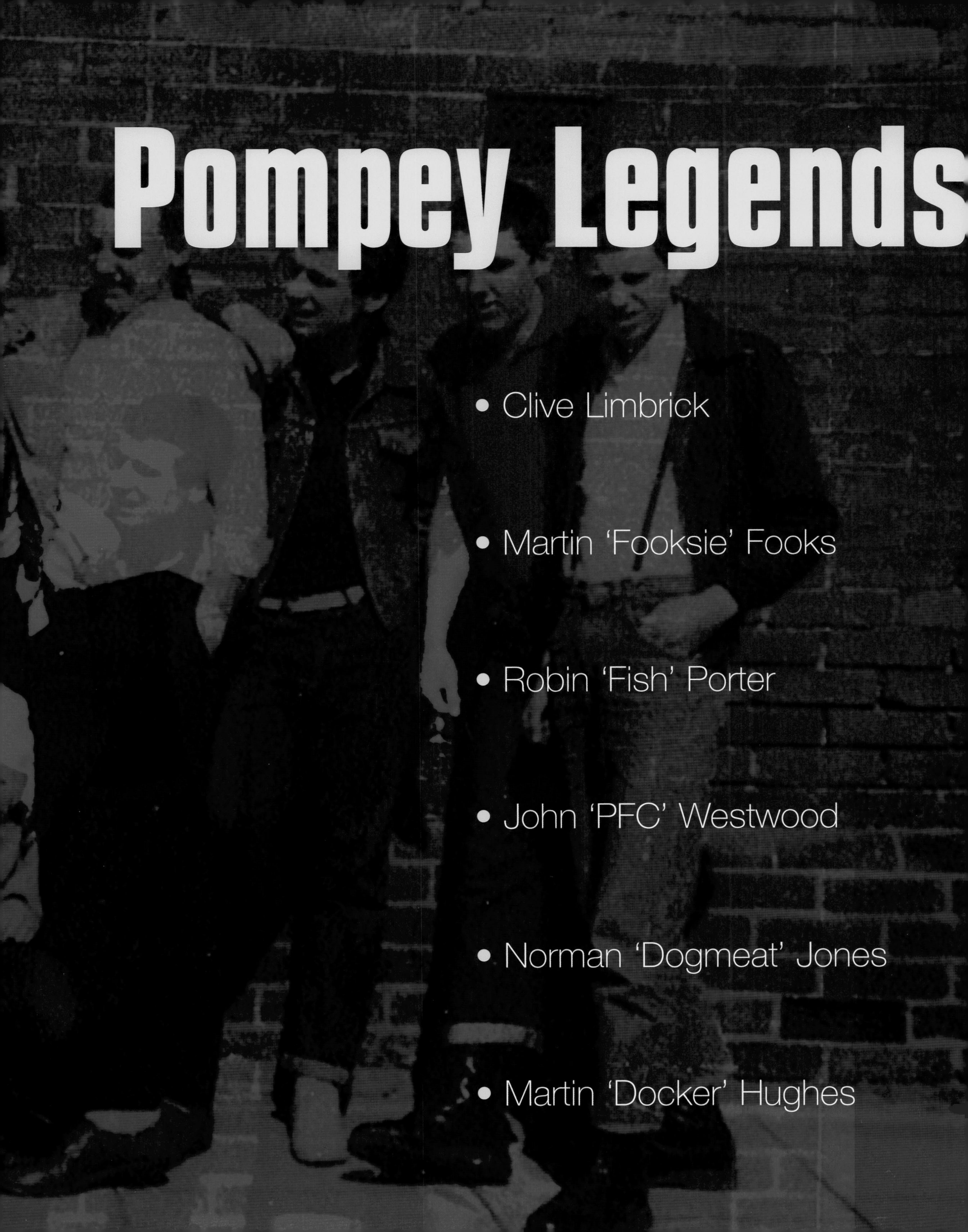

Pompey Legends

- Clive Limbrick

- Martin 'Fooksie' Fooks

- Robin 'Fish' Porter

- John 'PFC' Westwood

- Norman 'Dogmeat' Jones

- Martin 'Docker' Hughes

Clive Limbrick

Clive was an easy man to spot at a Pompey game, with his mop of ginger hair and his trademark sheepskin coat.

Clive ran coaches to away games from the infamous Leigh Park pub The Fox.

The passengers caused havoc wherever they travelled and built a reputation for being some of Pompey's toughest fans.

Clive was a true blue and followed the team all over the country even after they dropped through the leagues.

He died at a young age in 1980 but will be remembered by all that knew him as a top bloke and Pompey through and through.

Martin 'Fooksie' Fooks

Fooksie started running coaches to away games from the now defunct Monckton pub in Copnor Road in the Mid 70's. He ran a coach to all away games even through the dark days of the old 4th division.

He then chartered 'Football Special' trains to take Pompey fans all over the country following their team. The specials became legendary and anyone that went on such trips to Wigan, Hull or Lincoln will have fond memories. He even arranged to have KFC and football mail's delivered to the train on route from various Northern outpost's. If anyone wanted him on a train he would always be found in the guard's van conducting a card school.

In 1979 he even tried chartering a boat to take Pompey fans along the coast for an away match at Bournemouth. Would this have been the first time that any fans had travelled to an away match in England on a ferry? Unfortunately the Police stopped it running.

Fooksie's catch phrase for Pompey fans was 'keep the faith' and he still follows the Blues.

John 'PFC' Westwood

'Westy' AKA John Anthony Portsmouth Football Club Westwood has become one of the most recognised fans in football. He has missed only a handful of games over the last twenty years and his loyalty to the club has no equal.

He is a real character and has come to symbolize Pompey's passionate support.

Robin 'Fish' Porter

'Fish' was a well known character in the city, though he could usually be found around North End and Stamshaw. Whenever I saw him he would always be wearing moccasins even in mid-winter.

He followed Pompey all over the country and was respected by all for being as game as they come.

His antic's became legendary, following a court appearance in 1981 when asked his name in court he replied 'My name is Fish and I live in a dish, I ain't got time to pay my fine.'

Fish sadly died in 1994, but has gone down in Portsmouth folklore.

Norman 'Dogmeat' Jones

Dogmeat is another Leigh Parker who gained a reputation for being fearless even when the odds were stacked against him.

He became known for rousing renditions of the song 'Alouette'. Dogmeat would stand on a barrier or the side of the pitch and lead the Pompey fans in full voice. This was a standard Pompey song of the 70's and would bring many a laugh at away games especially from the local constabulary.

Dogmeat once told me that he had been to 87 different grounds following Pompey and all of them before opening time.

He is still an avid follower of The Blues.

ALOUETTE

Alouette, gentile Alouette
Alouette, je te plumerai.

Oh, I loved her one glass eye (oh, I loved her one glass eye)
The Alouette, (the Alouette), the Alouette, (the Alouette)

Alouette, gentile Alouette
Alouette, je te plumerai.

Oh, I loved her broken nose (oh, I loved her broken nose)
Her one glass eye (her one glass eye)
The Alouette, (the Alouette)

Alouette, gentile Alouette
Alouette, je te plumerai.

Oh, I loved her goofy teeth (oh, I loved her goofy teeth)
Her one glass eye (her one glass eye)
Her broken nose (her broken nose)
The Alouette, (the Alouette)

Alouette, gentile Alouette
Alouette, je te plumerai.

Oh, I loved her knobbly knees (oh, I loved her knobbly knees)
Her one glass eye (her one glass eye)
Her broken nose (her broken nose)
Her goofy teeth (her goofy teeth)
The Alouette, (the Alouette)

Repeat

Pigeon toes, massive tits, sweaty minge, shitty arse.

Martin 'Docker' Hughes

Docker is a true Pompey legend, if you met him in the street he would always be dressed in his full length leather coat with a rolled up sporting life in his pocket and a carrier bag in his hand. He would be the first to admit that he wasn't a 'face' but was known by everyone who followed Pompey home and away.

Docker got his 15 minutes of fame when in 1987 he stood in the parliamentary elections for the seat of Portsmouth South as the candidate for the 657 party. Supporters went around the city canvassing for votes. This included a tour on an open top bus with the rallying call 'Vote Docker'. On election night in the Guildhall the votes were counted and Docker has amassed a grand total of 455. Conservative candidate, David Martin, had beaten the Liberal Alliance candidate, Mike Hancock, by only 205 votes to become the Member of Parliament. Hancock was not a happy bunny and the story made local and national news.

Another Docker highlight was the 'Prize fight' with Waddle in the 5 a side pitches at Somerstown. The crowd turned out to see Milton's finest in action but he went down in a blaze of glory after 1 minute. Docker died suddenly in 1992, a crowd of over 300 turned out for his funeral including many Pompey players.

He is still remembered by all the lads and The Docker Hughes Memorial race is run every year at Fontwell racecourse.

PARLIAMENTARY ELECTIONS
Portsmouth South Constituency 1987

11 June 1987		Votes	
GARDINER, Keith	(LAB)	7047	
HANCOCK, Michael Thomas	(ALL)	23329	
HUGHES, Martin Ronald **known as 'Docker'**	**(657)**	**455**	
MARTIN, David John Pattison	(CON)	23534	**ELECTED**

David John Pattison Martin was declared duly elected to serve as the Member of Parliament for Portsmouth South.

Docker Hughes

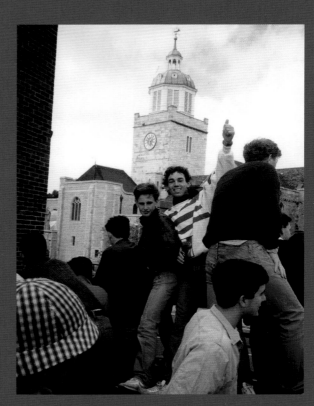

Docker Hughes

Tributes at Docker's funeral